SPEED, STRENGTH, AND STAMINA

Conditioning for Tennis

by Connie Haynes
with Eve Kraft and John Conroy

UNITED STATES LAWN TENNIS ASSOCIATION

TENNIS INSTRUCTIONAL SERIES

Illustrations by George Janes

DOUBLEDAY & COMPANY, INC.
GARDEN CITY, NEW YORK
1975

Library of Congress Cataloging in Publication Data

Haynes, Connie.
  Speed, strength, and stamina: conditioning for tennis.

  (Tennis instructional series)
  Bibliography: p. 93
  1. Tennis. 2. Exercise. I. Kraft, Eve, joint author. II. Conroy, John,
1908–   joint author. III. Title. IV. Series.
GV995.H39   796.34′22
ISBN 0-385-09758-1 Trade
      0-385-06981-2 Paperbound
Library of Congress Catalog Card Number 74–12691

Contents

Preface

If you're an average tennis player, you probably feel you're slower, weaker, and more tired than you'd like to be during many of your tennis matches. Read the following pages, pick the exercise plan that's right for you, and stay with it for eight weeks. You should come closer to your potential level of play.

If you're a tennis instructor, use this book as a guide for incorporating conditioning exercises into your tennis classes.

If you're an advanced player, there are conditioning plans especially for you. They can help you attain and maintain peak condition, indispensable for tournament play.

Perhaps you wonder what and when to eat before a big match. Or perhaps you're uncertain about the relationship between fatigue and glucose; salt and cramps. Answers to these and other related questions are given here, along with suggestions for emergency treatment of cramps, sprains, and fractures.

Finally, there's an underlying motive behind the book. Regular vigorous, sustained exercise like tennis builds endurance. It helps make your heart and lungs more efficient, helps keep your weight down, and improves your sense of well-being. And while most of us can't get to the courts every day, there is little to stop us from daily exercise except our own inertia and perhaps lack of a well-defined exercise plan. Hopefully, this book will inspire you to make regular, sustained exercise a daily habit. You will not only be fit for tennis, but fit for life.

The Australian champion, Margaret Court, who bounds about tennis courts with speed and agility, is a perfect example of what conditioning exercises can accomplish. Like most Australians, Margaret feels early and continued emphasis on physical fitness has been her primary key to success.

When Margaret was a child, her coach wanted her to run more swiftly and bend her knees more to get down to the ball, so he suggested that she run every day through the fields of the Australian countryside, picking daisies and tossing them aside. The Picking up "Daisies" exercise is one she has never abandoned, and you'll find it here, along with most of her other favorites.

Margaret's superb level of fitness, attained through rigorous training and self-discipline, is what has enabled her to return to the tournament circuit in peak, winning condition even after childbirth. Her often-quoted belief that "Many people know how to stroke the ball, but few know how to move to the ball" is one of the major sources of inspiration for this book.

SPEED, STRENGTH, AND STAMINA

I

Why Exercise?

Indeed, why exercise? Any tennis enthusiast will answer because it's fun to chase down a fuzzy, seamed, and dotted ball and attack it with a tennis racket. It's gratifying to hit a good, solid shot. And the satisfaction one feels results as much from sending problems and excess energy over the net with the ball as from winning the point. After a good workout on the courts, one feels pounds lighter and happier, more able to cope with the demands of everyday life.

Most tennis players recognize the pleasure tennis gives. It's an opportunity to be with friends, to bask in the sun, to sharpen our competitive wits against another person in an acceptable fashion. And—subconsciously—players know that tennis is contributing to their physical fitness in a way that bowling or golf probably never can or will. But why is exercise—especially vigorous, sustained exercise like tennis—good?

Recent studies indicate that lack of exercise is one of the major causes of heart disease. A regular exercise program which builds stamina has been found to play a role in the prevention of clinical coronary heart disease. Endurance exercise can also delay the onset of heart disease symptoms, or help one to survive a heart attack. Since so many thousands of Americans die each year from coronary heart disease, it would be important to exercise even if it weren't fun.

There are several ways in which exercise like tennis can help protect Americans from the ravages of coronary heart disease. Over a period of time, regular exercise makes the heart more efficient. Each stroke of the heart pumps more blood and delivers more oxygen to the cells, and as a result the resting heart rate is decreased. A slow, efficient heart is highly desirable, for a resting heart rate below 80 beats per minute has been directly associated with longevity.

One of the most important beneficial effects of exercise is an increase in collateral (small blood vessel) circulation in the heart muscle. If a large blood vessel does become obstructed, the blood flow through collateral vessels can mean the difference between life and death. One study noted that among men suffering an initial heart attack, those who habitually had the least physical activity had a mortality rate three times greater than those who exercised most.

Regular exercise has also been found by some investigators to decrease the blood pressure in people with slightly abnormal readings. Vigorous activity also temporarily lowers blood cholesterol and triglyceride levels, high levels of which have been closely tied to heart disease.

Obesity, long linked with heart disease, can be attacked with exercise as well as diet. A regular exercise program helps attain and maintain ideal weight, using up the extra calories which otherwise turn to fat.

Another physiological effect of exercise is the increased excretion of catecholamines. These are the very active by-products of our adrenalin metabolism and are responsible for increasing the blood pressure and pulse. If circulating in large enough quantities, they can cause extra heartbeats, general irritability, and gastro-intestinal disorders. We're much better off getting rid of them through exercise rather than allowing them to build up in our bloodstreams.

Although a sense of well-being can't be measured, exercise contributes immensely to that feeling. Simultaneously, psychic tension dwindles and often disappears.

All of these benefits from regular, sustained exercise can be summed up this way: Exercise improves fitness for life. If physically fit, one is able to perform at his top level of efficiency, without undue fatigue—at home, at work, and on the tennis courts. If fit, one consequently has good cardiopulmonary reserves to call upon in an emergency. Running for a train, shoveling snow, or having to play a third set in a tournament match on a 90-degree day all demand top physical condition. A regular exercise program can be a major factor in assuring that one is able to respond adequately to all the vicissitudes of life.

A SPECIAL NOTE FOR ADULTS

You really should consult your physician before launching a rigorous conditioning program. He may want to do an electrocardiogram, or even an exercise electrocardiogram, to be sure your cardiovascular system can handle vigorous exercise. You'll feel better having his OK.

Also, if you stop exercising for more than a week, don't try to do as much as you were doing before. Be patient with yourself. Build up gradually. Whether it takes eight weeks or much longer to get in shape is not as important as sticking with it day by day.

If you stop exercising for three weeks, begin at the beginning—you'll no longer be conditioned.

As you can see, it's better not to stop!

II

A Word to Instructors

Each exercise is included because it seems the simplest and best, without additional equipment, to achieve either speed, strength, or stamina. Some good exercises were eliminated from "on-court" plans because girls and ladies might find them awkward in a mixed group, while others are only in "off-court" plans because they would probably be too uncomfortable on a hard or hot court.

The time required for each exercise is approximate—try to move from one exercise to another without pause.

Studies have shown that it is those adults who had a regular program of exercise as children who are most likely to exercise as adults. If you can motivate your students to develop the habit of daily exercise, you'll be doing them a lasting favor. For example, you can:

1. Point to the increased self-assurance, especially in their game, that results from a firm, fit body.
2. Emphasize that the self-discipline required for daily exercise will spill over into other areas, contributing to an orderly mind as well as a trained body.
3. Have fun! Show by your enthusiastic example in group classes and varsity team practice that these exercises can be exhilarating rather than exhausting.
4. Use group games where possible to increase the group's enjoyment. Demonstrate that lively, fast-paced conditioning drills can be a pleasurable part of tennis.

The following diagrams may help you handle a large group doing exercises together:

Players in "open formation" for calisthenics:

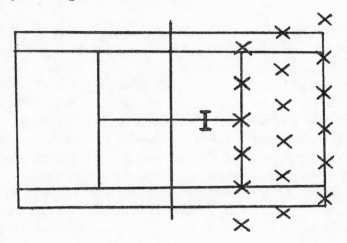

Players in line formation for relay races to practice footwork:

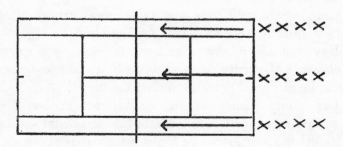

III

Beyond Strokes and Strategy:

Speed, Strength, and Stamina

There are several traits which should be developed in tennis players:

Range of motion, or flexibility—

So you can, without pulling a ligament, reach for the 90 per cent of shots which don't find you waiting in perfect ready position.

Quickness, or mobility—

So you can race to the baseline faster than a lob over your head and dash back to the net to retrieve the drop shot which follows.

Strength of hand, forearm, legs, and abdomen—

So you can hold on to the racket through three tough sets, and still have power for winning forehand drives;

So you can run from side to side, up and back, again and again, without your knees turning to rubber and your calves to clay;

So you can do a leaping scissor kick when you snap an overhead smash at your opponent's feet.

Cardiovascular endurance—

So you can continue playing well in the third set of a tournament match when it's 90 degrees and so humid your racket is sweating.

These traits can be represented by three "s's": speed, strength, and stamina. They are the bedrock upon which the skills and strategy that make up a good tennis player can be built.

Of course, if you play tennis every day, or even every other day, you'll gradually acquire more speed, strength, and stamina. But if you want to develop these traits to enhance your tennis, rather than as a slow by-product of your tennis, you need specific conditioning exercises. This book contains conditioning plans for several ability levels, carefully designed to help you achieve speed, strength, and stamina. They can help you overcome the conviction that your body is getting in the way of your superior mental game.

Perhaps you're agile and supple, but can't last through two sets of singles without exhaustion—exercises for stamina are included in each exercise plan. Or you can play for hours but have trouble running quickly enough to be a good retriever—each exercise plan contains exercises selected specifically to develop speed. If your legs, abdominal muscles, hand or arm are weak, the strengthening exercises which are part of each plan should bring noticeable results. The key is to exercise regularly, frequently, and progressively until you've reached your goal.

Most of the exercises in this book will be familiar to

anyone who has done calisthenics; they've been drawn from a variety of sources. Weight-lifting exercises were not included because a weight-lifting program should be done only under the close supervision of a professional trainer. Other popular exercises were eliminated because they required pulleys or other equipment not readily available, or because potential injury outweighed possible benefits.

Remember as you exercise that breathing is very important. Don't hold your breath; rather, breathe deeply and regularly throughout the exercises.

Another helpful hint: always warm up properly before exercising strenuously. A good series of warm-ups is included with each conditioning plan, but any gentle stretching exercises will get the blood flowing to large muscle groups and help avoid injury. This is especially important if you're going to play indoors during the winter months. The cold weather can make your muscles and joints stiffen up, and if you race onto the court and begin lunging about without proper warm-up, you're likely to pull your plantaris muscle and will be off the court and onto crutches in short order. So get there ten minutes early and warm up properly.

Cool down sufficiently, too. A couple of minutes of slow jogging or walking helps your system adjust to the sudden cessation of vigorous activity.

IV

Daily Exercise as a Habit:

Eight-week Conditioning Plans for All Ages and Abilities

The conditioning plans in the following chapters are designed for four major groups of tennis players:

1. Adults—beginner through advanced intermediate.
2. Junior and senior high school students—beginner through advanced intermediate.
3. Elementary school children—beginner through advanced intermediate.
4. Advanced players of all ages—interested in varsity level or tournament competition.

Within each group there is an on-court conditioning plan, for the days you play tennis, and an off-court conditioning plan, for the days you can't play tennis but still want to exercise.

You'll notice that each on-court conditioning plan consists of four parts:

1. Warm-ups.
2. Exercises to develop speed and strength.
3. Allowance for tennis playing, instruction, or practice time to develop racket-handling skills.
4. Stamina builders.

Although true circuit training hasn't been used in this book because it requires more space and supervision than will be available to most tennis players, a goal has been set for the number of times each exercise should be performed. You should be trying to reach that goal over an eight-week period, exercising daily.

For each group there are several alternatives within the main plans, and to the main plans, which will hopefully give the flexibility needed to fit exercise into varying life styles. Warm-ups and a tournament match may be substituted for either an on-court or an off-court conditioning plan.

Of course, there are variations in physical fitness among tennis players, and you must judge what you can do comfortably. Begin there. If you find the exercises easy, do more within the time allowed. If they seem difficult, pace yourself accordingly. And if you don't do the planned exercises at least every other day, do the exercises fewer times when returning to the plans so you won't strain yourself.

Be sure to do the exercises in the correct sequence. And remember that the exercises for stamina are placed at the end of each plan for a definite reason: to apply the principle of overloading. When output beyond that needed in match play is required, reserves of energy are created which will be available in a long match. The exercise done when you're already tired is that which increases your endurance.

Once you've reached your goal, continue at that level every day, or move to another plan when you become a more advanced player.

Although these conditioning plans can't guarantee that you'll hit backhands like Chris Evert, overheads like Margaret Court, serves like Jimmy Connors, or play with the cunning of Bobby Riggs, daily exercise is sure to make you look and feel better on and off the court.

V

Conditioning Plans for Adults
Beginners Through Advanced Intermediates

PLAN A—AN ON-COURT CONDITIONING PLAN

1. WARM-UPS (2 MINUTES)

These are recommended especially for group classes, to help students take conditioning seriously. They gently stretch the muscles and get the blood flowing to large muscle groups, making the transition to more strenuous exercise easier and safer. In each case, do a total of 15, with left and right counting as 1.

Pinwheel Technique: Stand straight, feet slightly apart, arms out at sides at shoulder height. Bend forward and try to touch left foot with right hand, keeping knees straight. Stand straight again and repeat, with left hand touching right foot. Remember to stretch rather than bob while performing this and other warm-ups.

Calf Stretch Technique: Place fingers on a shoulder-high support at arm's length. Keeping feet firmly on the floor, touch your nose to the support and push with your fingers to an upright position.

Warm-ups make the transition to more strenuous exercises

easier and faster.

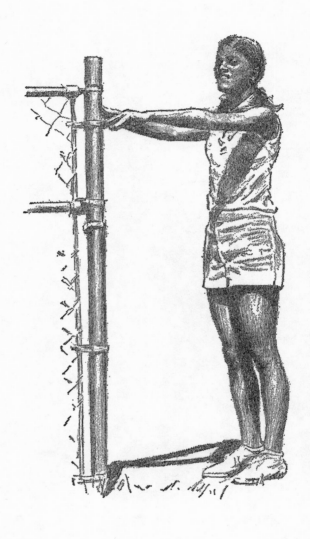

The Calf Stretch gently stretches the backs of the legs, help-

ing to prevent pulled muscles and torn ligaments.

Sidewinder Technique: Stand straight, feet slightly apart. Keeping back straight, bend to the left, reaching as far down left leg as possible. Stand straight again and repeat to the right.

Windmill Technique: Stand straight, feet slightly apart, arms at sides. With both arms, make large circles backward and around, then reverse and do forward circles.

2. EXERCISES FOR SPEED AND STRENGTH (2 MINUTES)

"Quickness has helped me out of many a tight spot."
                                        Ken Rosewall,
                                        Australian tennis pro

Loaded Net Rush and Backward Sprint Technique: With racket cover on, and racket in ready position, run up to net and then run backward to baseline as fast as you can, 3 times.
Value: Develops speed in running forward and backward, and makes racket feel lighter during play.

Loaded Net Rush and Simulated Volley Technique: With racket cover on, and racket in ready position, run to net and simulate the volley, moving racket as quickly as possible from forehand to backhand, 3 times.
Value: Helps develop speed and agility in performing the volley, and helps develop arm strength.

Exercises done with a racket cover on, such as the Loaded
Net Rush and Simulated Volley, make the racket feel lighter
during actual play.

The use of a weighted racket in the Simulated Forehand and

Backhand helps develop quickness and increases arm strength.

Simulated Forehand and Backhand Technique: Assume ready position, holding racket weighted with racket cover. Pivot and take crossover step with left foot while you execute forehand stroke. Return to ready position as quickly as possible, pivot and crossover with right foot, quickly simulating backhand stroke, 5 times.

Value: Helps develop speedy forehand and backhand strokes while increasing arm strength.

Simulated Overhead Technique: Assume ready position, holding racket weighted with racket cover. Run backward a few steps, leap into the air, and make an imaginary overhead smash, 5 times.

Value: Helps you to be agile in performing the overhead smash.

Racket Press Technique: Two players face each other. Press the face of your racket against the face of your partner's racket, contracting your arm muscles and counting to 6. Relax and repeat with backhand, 5 times in 1 minute.

Value: An isometric exercise which strengthens arm muscles.

3. INSTRUCTION OR PRACTICE OR PLAYING TIME— SKILL BUILDERS

This is the time to work on specific racket handling skills and strategy. It's left open so this plan can be used in a class situation, or by friends going to practice what they've learned in class. Though the time spent on this part of the plan will vary, what should remain constant is its placement in the plan—after the warm-ups and exercises for speed and strength, before the exercise for stamina.

4. EXERCISE FOR STAMINA

No running is *required* for adults at this level in the "on-court" plan, particularly if the plan is used as part of an instructional program, because many adults will be tired by the time the class is drawing to a close. They may also feel further running is a waste of class time. However, if you as an individual want to increase your stamina, you should know that running is universally recommended as the best conditioner for your heart and lungs. An easy jog around the tennis courts, an open field, or a gym is a fine way to finish up this plan if you feel up to it.

"No one knows what he can do until he tries."
Maxim 786

Plan B—AN OFF-COURT CONDITIONING PLAN

These exercises are invaluable as home practice—
or even for an instructional class on a rainy day when
a gym or limited facilities are necessary. The warm-ups
in this plan do not change from Plan A, so that players
will become accustomed to doing the same warm-ups
whether they are on the court or at home, and will more
easily develop the habit of daily exercise.

1. WARM-UPS (2 MINUTES)
SAME AS PLAN A.

2. EXERCISES FOR SPEED AND STRENGTH
(3 MINUTES AND 30 SECONDS)

Skip Rope Technique: Begin by skipping rope at a
moderate pace for 1 minute. Try to gradually increase
the skipping pace, until you can do at least 60 skips
per minute.
Value: Especially good for speedy footwork. Also contributes to co-ordination and leg strength.

Double Leg Raise Technique: Lie on back with legs
straight in front of body, arms locked under head.
Slowly raise both legs off the floor, about 18 inches,
keeping legs straight. Slowly lower legs to floor. Do
15 in about 1 minute.
Value: Strengthens abdominal muscles.

Skipping Rope is one of the best all-round conditioners. Gradually work up to 60 skips per minute to develop speedy footwork, co-ordination, and leg strength.

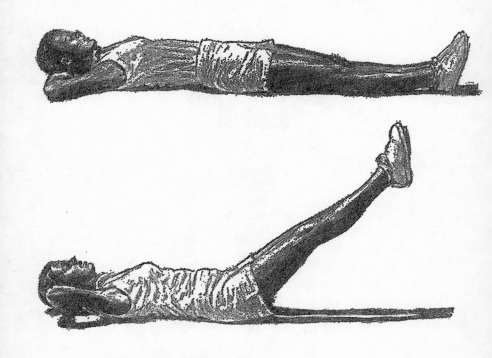

Double Leg Raises develop strong abdominal muscles, so necessary for overheads, and a good indicator of fitness.

Ball Squeeze   Technique: Squeeze a tennis ball as tightly as possible with the racket hand for about 6 seconds, contracting the stomach muscles. Relax for 6 seconds and repeat, 5 times.
Value: Strengthens hand and arm muscles.

Bench Step   Technique: Place one foot on a low bench. Step up with other foot to that step. Lower the first foot to the original position, and then lower other foot. Continue for 30 seconds, changing lead foot after 15 seconds.
Value: Strengthens large muscles in front of thighs.

OR

Bicycle Riding   Technique: Sit on floor, legs straight in front of body, heels about an inch above the floor. Bring one knee to chest and then quickly extend leg straight while bringing other knee to chest. Continue alternating knees to chest for 1 minute, counting left and right as one, for a total of 50.
Value: Strengthens abdominal muscles.

Newspaper Crumple   Technique: Grasp a large single sheet of newspaper at one corner. Holding it at arm's length, straight out in front of body, try to crumple the paper into a small ball, using one hand.
Value: Strengthens hand and forearm muscles.

Bicycle Riding is another excellent exercise for strengthening abdominal muscles.

Starts Technique: Assume push-up position. Bring left leg forward between hands, then quickly return left leg to starting position while bringing right leg forward. Do 30 in 1 minute, counting only left leg.

Value: Helps to give you a quicker start to the ball.

3. EXERCISE FOR STAMINA

Run or jog 1 mile in 8 minutes. Work up to this *gradually*—you may want to begin by jogging only 1 minute, or if you've been exercising regularly you may be able to do a lot more from the beginning. Over an eight-week period, slowly increase the distance, the pace, or both, until you've reached your goal. You'll be amazed at how quickly you'll recover after strenuous points in a match.

Alternate Plans Substitute any one of these for Plan A or Plan B.

Walk or bike 2 miles to work, bus, or train and home again.

OR

Ski, swim, or participate in any other sport which requires at least half an hour of sustained and moderately vigorous activity.

OR

Warm-ups and a tournament match.

"When you're past 30 bulging biceps and pleasing pectorals may boost your ego, but your life and health may depend on how fit your heart and lungs are."

W. E. Harris, M.D., author of *Jogging*.

VI

Conditioning Plans for Junior and Senior High School Students

Beginners Through Advanced Intermediates

Plan A—AN ON-COURT CONDITIONING PLAN

1. WARM-UPS (2 MINUTES)

These stretching exercises get the blood flowing to large muscle groups, making the transition to more strenuous exercises easier and safer. They also contribute to flexibility.

Ferris Wheel   Technique: Stand straight with feet about 12 inches apart, hands clasped overhead. Bend to right, in circular fashion, and touch right foot, then left foot, and return to starting position to complete circle. Repeat, reversing direction halfway through total number of repetitions, for a total of 20.

Backward Leg Stretch   Technique: Hold on to a fence or other shoulder-high support. Lift each leg behind and up as far as possible and pull it even farther up with your hand. Alternate legs, counting left and right as one, for a total of 15.

The Knee Hug contributes to flexibility. Like all warm-ups, it gently stretches the muscles and gets the blood flowing to large muscle groups.

Knee Hug Technique: Stand straight, hands at sides, feet together. Raise left knee and pull to chest with hands, keeping back straight. Repeat with right leg, and continue alternating knees to chest, for a total of 20.

Crisscross Technique: Stand straight, arms held out at sides parallel to floor. Swing arms to front and across each other, scissors fashion, and return to starting position. Keep repeating, with first right arm crossing above left, and then left arm crossing above right, for a total of 30.

2. EXERCISES FOR SPEED AND STRENGTH (3 MINUTES)

Picking up "Daisies" Technique: Place balls in a row, 5 to 10 feet apart. Running as fast as you can, pick up each ball and toss it aside. In class, do as a relay. About 1 minute.
Value: Develops speed in running and bending knees.

Ball Squeeze Technique: Squeeze a tennis ball as tightly as possible with the racket hand for about 6 seconds, contracting the stomach muscles. Relax for 6 seconds and repeat for a total of 5.
Value: Strengthens hand and forearm muscles.

The Picking up "Daisies" exercise, one of Margaret Court's favorites, is wonderful for developing speed in running and bending knees.

The Racket Jump is an excellent way to develop lateral mo-

bility and leg strength.

Racket Jump Technique: Place your racket on the floor. Stand beside it and jump over it sideways, landing in a semi-squat position. Jump back sideways, again landing with knees bent. Do 30 in 1 minute.

Value: Good for lateral mobility and leg strength.

OR

Shuttle Run Technique: Have two tennis balls or other points, A and B, 10 yards apart. Try to lower your time for running between A and B 10 times, or 100 yards. In class, do as a relay.

Value: Increases sprinting speed, so you can get to the ball quicker.

Racket Press Technique: Two students face each other. Press the face of your racket against the face of your partner's racket, contracting arm muscles and counting to 6. Relax and repeat with backhand, for a total of 5 times.

Value: Strengthens arm muscles.

Alternate Low Splitting Technique: Stand straight. Spring into the air and land with right foot forward and left foot back, knees bent. Spring and reverse landing. Do a total of 15 in 30 seconds.

Value: Strengthens legs.

3. INSTRUCTION OR PRACTICE OR PLAYING TIME—
SKILL BUILDERS

This is the time to work on specific racket handling skills and strategy. It's left open so this plan can be used in a class situation, or by friends going out to practice what they've learned in class. Though the time spent on this part of the plan will vary, what should remain constant is its placement in the plan—after the warm-ups and exercises for speed and strength, before the exercises for stamina.

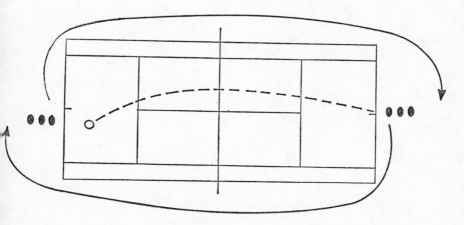

A group of students can have a lot of fun and build stamina too, playing Round-the-Court Knockout.

4. EXERCISES FOR STAMINA (5 MINUTES)

Round-the-Court Knockout Technique: Players stand behind the baseline and drive the ball to the opposite side using forehand or backhand drives. After hitting the ball, player runs around the outside of the court and goes to the end of the line on the opposite baseline. Players lose points for each error and are eliminated after a certain number of errors. May also be played with two teams.

Value: An excellent way for a group of students to work on building stamina—and to have fun in the process.

OR

Round-the-Court Jog Technique: Jog three times around the outside of three courts. Rest 30 seconds and repeat.

Value: An excellent stamina builder.

Plan B—AN OFF-COURT CONDITIONING PLAN

Especially meant for the days when you can't get to the courts. Also can be used in a gym on days when a class can't use the courts because of rain.

1. WARM-UPS (2 MINUTES)

The warm-ups are the same as Plan A to help players develop the habit of daily exercise.

2. EXERCISES FOR SPEED AND STRENGTH (2 MINUTES)

Skip Rope Technique: Skip rope, fast, for 1 minute, aiming for more than 60 skips.
Value: Excellent for footwork; also good for co-ordination and leg strength.

Push-ups Lie face down with hands under shoulders and palms flat on floor. Straighten arms, lifting body off floor supported by palms and toes. Keep back straight and be sure to touch floor with chest during each push-up. Girls may wish to do knee push-ups. Do 20 in about 30 seconds.
Value: Strengthens shoulder and arm muscles.

Strong legs are essential to good tennis. They can be developed

by exercises like the Single Knee Jump.

Sit-ups Technique: Lie on back with legs straight, feet together, and arms straight overhead. Sit up and touch toes, keeping legs straight. Return to starting position. Do 20 in 30 seconds.

Value: Strengthens abdominal, back, and front of thigh muscles.

OR

Single Knee Jump Technique: Stand with feet together. Bound up, pulling one knee to chest. Bound again, pulling other knee to chest. Keep alternating knees to chest, counting left and right as 1, for a total of 25 in 1 minute.

Value: Strengthens leg muscles.

Newspaper Crumple Technique: Grasp a large single sheet of newspaper at one corner. Holding it at arm's length, straight out in front of body, try to crumple the paper into a small ball, using one hand.

Value: Strengthens hand and forearm muscles.

Horizontal Double Leg Kick Technique: Lie on back with hands clasped behind head and legs extended about 12 inches off floor. Try to sit up and touch knees to chest, and then thrust legs forward as you return to starting position. Do 15 in 30 seconds.

Value: Strengthens abdominal and back muscles.

The Newspaper Crumple is a simple way to strengthen hand and forearm muscles.

The Horizontal Double Leg Kick strengthens abdominal and back muscles at the same time.

3. EXERCISE FOR STAMINA (12 MINUTES)

Gradually work up to jogging 1½ miles in 12 minutes, or run in place for 12 minutes. There really is no substitute for running, and you'll find that it will help you to recover very quickly after strenuous points in a match.

Alternate Plans May be substituted for either Plan A or Plan B. Walk or bike 1½ miles to school, participate in physical education class, walk or bike home.

OR

Swim; play basketball, hockey, lacrosse, or soccer; ski; run in a track program. Do gymnastics or cheerleading, or any other sport which requires at least half an hour of sustained, vigorous activity.

OR

Warm-ups and a tournament match.

"You may have the greatest strokes in the world, but you won't be able to hit them very well if you're tired."

Rod Laver, Australian tennis pro

VII

Conditioning Plans for Elementary School Children

Beginners Through Advanced Intermediates

PLAN A—AN ON-COURT CONDITIONING PLAN

1. WARM-UPS (2 MINUTES)

For stretching and loosening up the muscles.

Pinwheel Technique: Stand straight, feet slightly apart, arms out at sides at shoulder height. Bend forward and try to touch left foot with right hand, keeping knees straight. Stand straight again and repeat, with left hand touching right foot. Remember to stretch rather than bob while performing this and other warm-ups. Do a total of 10, with left and right counting as 1.

Knee Hug Technique: Stand straight, hands at sides, feet together. Raise left knee and pull to chest with hands, keeping back straight. Repeat with right leg, and continue alternating knees to chest. Do a total of 10, with left and right counting as 1.

The Pinwheel and other warm-ups gently stretch and loosen

the muscles, getting them ready for more strenuous exercises or play.

Sidewinder Technique: Stand straight, feet slightly apart. Keeping back straight, bend to left, reaching as far down left leg as possible. Stand straight again and repeat to the right. Do a total of 10, with left and right as 1.

Windmill Technique: Stand straight, feet slightly apart, arms at sides. With both arms, make 10 large circles backward and around, then reverse and do 10 forward circles.

2. EXERCISES FOR SPEED AND STRENGTH (3 MINUTES)

Potato Race Technique: Put a bucket down, and scatter ten tennis balls in a circle at distances between 6 and 12 yards from the bucket. Run to retrieve each ball and run back to put it in the bucket. Keep running until all the balls are in the bucket. Try to increase your speed each time you do this race. About 1½ minutes.
Value: Develops speed in running and bending knees.

Jumping Jacks Technique: Stand with arms at sides, feet together. Jump up and land with feet apart, clapping hands, and jump back to starting position. Repeat, for a total of 30 in 30 seconds.
Value: Good for co-ordination and agility; also helps develop leg strength.

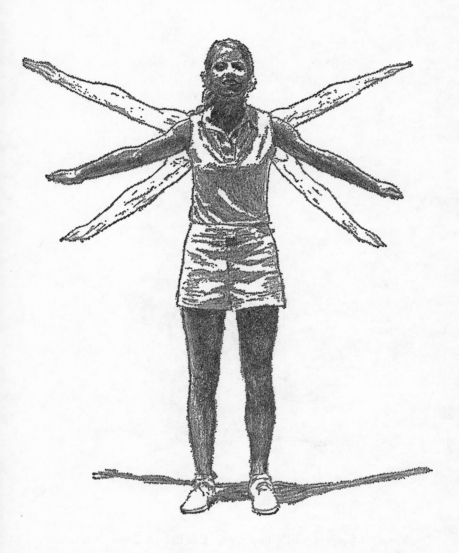

The Windmill is a good exercise to do before serving practice, as well as part of this conditioning plan.

Younger players will enjoy doing the Potato Race as a relay. The first person on each team can retrieve the balls, and the second can scatter them, always remembering to place rather than throw each ball.

Hand Press Technique: Two students face each other, palms pressed against one another with wrists locked. They contract their arm and body muscles tightly as they count to 6 and then relax. Repeat, pressing the back of the palms against one another, for a total of 5 times.

Value: Builds strength in the hand and arm.

3. INSTRUCTION OR PRACTICE OR PLAYING TIME— SKILL BUILDERS

This is the time to work on specific racket handling skills and strategy. It's left open so this plan can be used in a class situation, or by friends going out to practice what they've learned in class. Though the time spent on this part of the plan will vary, what should remain constant is its placement in the plan—after the warm-ups and exercises for speed and strength, before the exercises for stamina.

4. EXERCISES FOR STAMINA (6 MINUTES)

Wind Sprints Technique: Run around the outside of three courts, jogging the sidelines, sprinting the baselines.

OR

Skip Rope Technique: Skip at a regular, even pace until you are tired; then continue skipping for a total of six minutes.

Value: One of the best conditioners if continued beyond the point of initial fatigue.

Skipping Rope is one of the best conditioners there is. For maximum effect, skip rope beyond the point of initial fatigue.

Plan B—AN OFF-COURT CONDITIONING PLAN

1. WARM-UPS (2 MINUTES)

The warm-ups are the same as Plan A to help players more easily develop the habit of daily exercise.

2. EXERCISES FOR SPEED AND STRENGTH (3 MINUTES)

Double-legged Treadmill Technique: Assume push-up position. Bring both feet between hands and extend to original position. Do 25 in 1 minute.

Scissors on Floor Technique: Lie flat on back, hands behind head, legs held about 12 inches off the floor and straight. Make a scissoring motion with your legs, spreading them wide and crossing them while keeping knees straight. Do 15 in 30 seconds.

Racket Pull Technique: Hold racket at arms length, chin high, with handle pointed toward the floor. Grasp the sides of the frame with a hand on each side and try to pull arms sideward as if tearing the frame apart. Relax and repeat. Do 3 in 30 seconds.

The Double-legged Treadmill starts from a push-up position. Its primary effect is to increase leg strength, but it's also good for arms and abdomen.

3. EXERCISE FOR STAMINA

Jog—in your room, around your yard, or around the block. Try to keep jogging for 8 minutes, or about 1 mile.

Alternate Plans To be substituted for Plan A or Plan B. Walk or bike 1½ miles to school. Take part in physical education class at school. Walk or bike home.

OR

Swim; play basketball, hockey, or soccer; ski; do gymnastics or any other sport that uses your muscles continuously over half an hour and leaves you tired.

OR

Warm-ups and a two-out-of-three-set tournament match.

VIII

Conditioning Plans for Advanced Players (Juniors and Adults)

Interested in Varsity-level or Tournament Competition

PLAN A—AN ON-COURT CONDITIONING PLAN

1. WARM-UPS (2 MINUTES)

These stretching exercises increase flexibility and get the blood flowing to large muscle groups, making the transition to more strenuous exercise easier and safer.

Backward Leg Stretch   Technique: Hold on to a fence or other shoulder-high support. Lift each leg behind and up as far as possible and pull it up even farther with your hand. Alternate legs, with left and right counting as 1, for a total of 18.

Side Stretch   Technique: Lie on your side with legs straight, both arms stretched over head along floor. Have someone hold your feet down, and raise your upper body sideways. Turn over and repeat, raising other side. Count each side stretch as 1 and do a total of 12.

Side Leg Lifts Technique: Lie on your side with legs straight, lower arm straight under head and other arm used for balance. Raise your upper leg straight up as far as possible and then lower it. Then turn over and raise other leg the same way. Count left and right as 1 and do a total of 26.

Swallow Technique: Lie on stomach, with someone holding your feet down if possible. With hands behind head, raise upper body as far as possible. Do 10.

2. EXERCISES FOR SPEED AND STRENGTH (3 MINUTES)

"A hard, dependable body produces a cool, confident state of mind."

Frank Sedgman, Australian tennis pro

Sprint and Crossover Technique: Sprint 10 yards, come to a "split" stop, lunge to the right with a crossover step, and return to ready position. Repeat by sprinting 10 yards and lunging to the left. Do a total of 6, three to the right and three to the left, in 30 seconds.
Value: Good for quickness, mobility, and stretching.

Push-ups Technique: Lie face down with hands under shoulders and palms flat on floor. Straighten arms, lifting body off floor supported by palms and toes. Keep back straight, and be sure to touch floor with chest during each push-up. Girls may wish to start with knee

push-ups, done the same way except body supported
by palms and knees. Do 30 in 30 seconds.
Value: Strengthens shoulder and arm muscles.

Spot Run Technique: Run in place, fast, raising knees.
Do 100 steps in 1 minute, counting only left foot.
Value: Excellent for quickness and leg strength.

Simulated Overhead Technique: Assume ready position, holding racket weighted with racket cover. Run
backward a few steps, leap into the air, and make an
imaginary overhead smash. Do 5 in 30 seconds.
Value: Helps you to be agile in performing the overhead smash, and makes racket feel lighter during
match play.

Kangaroo Hops Technique: Stand on toes with feet together. Leap up, bound knees against chest, and return
to starting position. Do 30 in 30 seconds.
Value: Strengthens leg muscles.

OR

Lateral Spring Technique: Assume ready position.
Spring to the right, landing on your right foot and bending your knee. Without stopping, spring to your left foot
and bend that knee. Do 20 in 30 seconds.
Value: Helps develop lateral mobility.

The Spot Run can be done anywhere and is excellent for quickness and leg strength. Continued beyond the point of initial fatigue, it's an excellent conditioner for the heart and lungs.

The Kangaroo Hop is a strenuous leg strengthener and all-

round conditioner. You'll have to be in reasonably good condition to do even a few of these.

Arm Circling Technique: Stand with arms held out straight at shoulder height. Make small backward circles with arms, then gradually increase size of circles. Do 60 in 30 seconds.

Value: Strengthens posterior shoulder muscles.

Half Squat Technique: With back straight and arms extended straight in front, slowly lower body to half-squat position. Hold for several seconds and slowly return to standing position. Do 6 in 1 minute.

Value: Strengthens large muscles in the front of the thighs.

Trunk Curl Technique: Lie flat on back, hands clasped behind head. While keeping legs straight, bend up to touch knees with forehead. Do 30 in 1 minute.

Value: Strengthens abdominal and back muscles.

3. INSTRUCTION OR PRACTICE OR PLAYING TIME— SKILL BUILDERS

This is the time to work on specific racket handling skills and strategy; it's left open so this plan can be used in a class situation, or by friends going out to practice what they've learned in class. Though the time spent on this part of the plan will vary, what should remain constant is it's placement in the plan—after the warm-ups and exercises for speed and strength, before the exercises for stamina.

The Half Squat is a simple, effective way to strengthen the large muscles in the front of the thighs.

4. EXERCISES FOR STAMINA (UNDER 8 MINUTES)

Wind Sprints Technique: Begin the first week by jogging 10 yards, sprinting 10 yards, and walking 10 yards, 5 times. Gradually eliminate walking and increase jogging and sprinting distances, until by the eighth week you are alternating 100 yards of jogging with 25-yard sprints, 10 times.

For example:

Week 1: jog 10 yards, sprint 10 yards, walk 10 yards
Week 2: jog 15 yards, sprint 10 yards, walk 5 yards
Week 3: jog 20 yards, sprint 10 yards
Week 4: jog 25 yards, sprint 10 yards
Week 5: jog 40 yards, sprint 15 yards
Week 6: jog 60 yards, sprint 20 yards
Week 7: jog 80 yards, sprint 20 yards
Week 8: jog 100 yards, sprint 25 yards

OR

Line Drill Technique: Divide a class of twenty into five teams of four players each. Players line up behind the doubles line with a pile of five balls at the head of each line. First player on each team picks up one ball, runs to the far singles line and *places* (not throws) the ball on that line. He then sprints back to his pile of balls, picks up the next ball, and places it on the far doubles line. He returns, picks up the third ball, and places it on the doubles line of the next court. The fourth ball is placed on the singles line of the next court, and the fifth on the far singles line of the next court. First team to finish wins.

Value: This drill, done at the end of a class, is an excellent way to build stamina. It also develops speed and quickness in bending knees.

OR

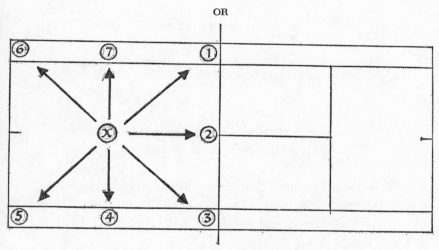

A class or team of advanced players will find the Squash Drill an enjoyable way to improve footwork, agility, and stamina.

Squash Drill Technique: Start from position x on the diagram. Use side shuffle and crossover steps to move clockwise around court. Shuffle up to position 1, touch the net pole with racket, return to x. Then move to position 2, and return to x. Move as in court play, and never turn your back to the net. Can be done against clock or as a relay race.

Value: Excellent for footwork, agility, and especially stamina when done at the end of a class with a group or team.

"Only work done when tired brings about any significant change in endurance."   Chet Murphy
                    Varsity Tennis Coach, University of California

Plan B—AN OFF-COURT CONDITIONING PLAN

1. WARM-UPS (2 MINUTES)

Same as Plan A, so players will more easily develop the habit of daily exercise.

2. EXERCISES FOR SPEED AND STRENGTH (3 MINUTES AND 30 SECONDS)

Hop-Chop Timing Technique: Stand straight. Jump up, reaching with both arms skyward. Then jump down, bending knees, and touch floor. Repeat for a total of 20 in 30 seconds.
Value: Helps develop mobility, especially for low volleys and overheads.

Push-ups Technique: Lie face down with hands under shoulders and palms flat on floor. Straighten arms, lifting body off floor supported by palms and toes. Keep back straight, and be sure to touch floor with chest during each push up. Girls may wish to start with knee push-ups, down the same way except with body supported by palms and knees. Do 30 in 30 seconds.
Value: Strengthens shoulder and arm muscles.

Skip Rope Technique: Skip rope, as fast as you can, for 1 minute.
Value: Excellent way to speedier footwork.

Triple Toe Touch Technique: Lie flat on back, legs about 24 inches apart, arms straight overhead. Keeping legs straight and on floor, sit up and touch first left foot, then floor between feet, and then right foot. Return to starting position and repeat, for a total of 25 in 1 minute.

Value: Strengthens abdominal muscles and helps make back and arm muscles more flexible.

Starts Technique: Assume push-up position. Bring left leg forward between hands, then quickly return left leg to starting position while bringing right leg forward. Do 25 in 30 seconds, counting left leg only.

Value: Helps to give you a quicker start to the ball.

OR

Star Jump Technique: Leap into the air, touching hands and toes up and in front of you, legs and arms straight. Do 30 in 1 minute.

Value: Strengthens leg muscles.

Push-ups Technique: Lie face down with hands under shoulders and palms flat on floor. Straighten arms, lifting body off floor supported by palms and toes. Keep back straight, and be sure to touch floor with chest during each push up. Girls may wish to do knee push-ups. Do 30 in 30 seconds.

Value: Strengthens shoulder and arm muscles.

Bench Jump Technique: Jump sideways over low bench, 30 times in 1 minute.

Value: Strengthens legs and aids lateral mobility.

Starts increase leg strength and help give you a quicker start to the ball.

The Star Jump is a difficult but excellent exercise for strengthening leg muscles.

The Bench Jump is an advanced version of the Racket Jump,

designed to strengthen legs and increase lateral mobility.

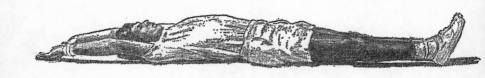

Strong abdominal and back muscles can be developed if you do Body Pikes regularly, frequently, and progressively.

Body Pikes Technique: Lie on back with arms extended overhead. Raise upper body and legs simultaneously and touch feet with fingers. Keep upper body and knees straight. Do 30 in 1 minute.
Value: Strengthens abdominal and back muscles.

3. EXERCISE FOR STAMINA

Jog—there is no substitute for it! Boys and men, work up to 3 miles a day; girls and women, aim for 2 miles. If this seems like a lot, remember that Roy Emerson, Australian tennis pro, runs 6 miles a day when he's in training. Running is the best conditioner for your heart and lungs and is *guaranteed* to improve your stamina on the court if you do it every day. Try it—you may not like it, but you'll like what it does for you.

Alternate Plans   May be substituted for Plan A or Plan B. Warm-ups and a two-out-of-three-set match, followed by a slow jog for 1 mile.

OR

Warm-ups and a tournament match.

"Practice is the best of all instructors."
Maxim 439

If you want to improve your stamina—jog! Daily jogging will help you sustain your top level of play through long matches.

The Care and Feeding of Tennis Players

is not really very different from the care and feeding of ordinary people. What is required mostly is common sense and a willingness to admit that your everyday habits greatly influence your physical condition. Treat your body intelligently and kindly, and it will perform for you.

Sleep is essential for a healthy body and a positive state of mind. You should feel rested when you get up in the morning.

Cigarettes should be thrown away. They turn your lungs black and make you huff and puff while your non-smoking opponent (who may be the same size, age, and weight) will still be going strong. If you're a smoker you won't be able to play good tennis—or any kind of tennis—very long.

Alcohol won't help your tennis, nor will it contribute to your fitness. Trying to play tennis with a hangover is like trying to catch a fish with your bare hands. It may be possible, but why bother? It's a waste of time.

Food fads come and go, but the basic nutritional requirements for optimum health have remained fairly steady for years. Tennis players should eat a balanced diet based on foods from the Basic Four: (1) milk and milk products (2) poultry, fish, and meat (3) fruits and vegetables (4) whole grain breads and cereals, keeping in mind that cardiologists recommend no more than four eggs a week and as little saturated fat as possible.
This means:

— Cut visible fat off meat.
— Use polyunsaturated margarine rather than butter, and polyunsaturated vegetable oil rather than lard or shortening.
— Avoid pastries and deep-fat fried foods as much as possible.
— Drink skim milk or buttermilk instead of whole milk.
— Increase the number of meals containing fish or poultry and decrease the number of meals containing meat.
— Save ice cream, cream cheese, chocolate, and candy for special occasions rather than as part of your daily diet.

If you need to lose weight, join Weight Watchers or one of the other reputable diet groups rather than going on a crash diet. For the athlete in competition, a stable diet and stepped-up exercise is recommended rather than a total protein diet, or fast, because strenuous activity requires readily available sugar, which the body cannot produce quickly enough from protein or fat. It must be supplied in the diet in the form of carbohydrates.

Before a Big Match   there are a few simple measures you can take which may make a tremendous difference in how you play. First, eat your breakfast, lunch, or dinner two to three hours before you step on the court. It should be a complete meal, high in carbohydrates, but should not contain large amounts of sugar, which will raise your blood sugar level quite high. This can trigger an increased flow of insulin, lowering your blood sugar and making you suddenly tired when you least want to be—just as you walk on the court. So don't begin the match with a full stomach —it will slow you down and may give you cramps.

If it's hot, take salt tablets with lots of water early in the day, 6–12 .3 gm tablets. Don't take them during a match, as they may make you nauseated. If you tend to be nervous in competition, stay away from coffee or other stimulants—instead of extra energy all you'll get will be the jitters. If you have any minor aches and pains, two buffered aspirin fifteen minutes before you begin can relieve them and help in the warming-up process. And while you're waiting for your court, do your exercises for warming up. They only take two minutes and may keep you from defaulting with a ruptured Achilles' tendon!

During the Match   remember that you'll be using up the sugar stored in your muscles (glycogen) and will feel fatigue in those muscles unless you replace that sugar. So you should have a ready source of sugar available: sugar cubes, orange juice, honey, dextrose wafers, or one of the commercially prepared beverages containing salt, potassium, and sugar. The latter are especially good because they closely resemble the composition of perspiration and can prevent dehydration from salt and potassium loss. Whatever you choose, sip it or munch it between games and sets, and if you're munching, drink water to quench your thirst. Remember, too, that it's not a good idea to sit for too long if you're going back on the court to play another set. Rest a couple of minutes, then get up and move around if there's a delay for any reason. Otherwise it may take you a couple of games to get back in stride.

FIRST AID

is something with which tennis players should be at least a little familiar. Temporary and immediate care of injuries until the tennis player can be seen by a physician can reduce the extent of injury and hasten recovery.

Sprained Ankles, Torn Muscles, and Ligaments   are fairly common, and should be seen by a physician. If possible, apply an ice bag or cold cloths immediately. Support the injured limb and obtain medical care.

Cramps   in the legs may be due to poor conditioning or to salt loss. Give sips of salt water or a commercially prepared beverage containing salt. This should give prompt relief, and if not, obtain medical care.

Blisters   should be covered with a loose Band-Aid or gauze dressing if not broken. If broken, the edges should be trimmed with sterile equipment and a bandage applied. An infected blister should receive medical care.

Nose Bleeds can usually be stopped by the application of ice-cold cloths to the nose and pressure at the sides of the nose. Have the player sit or stand rather than lie down. Again, call the doctor if bleeding persists.

Eyes can be injured by swinging rackets or by particles lodged in them. Apply ice to area around eye if it has received a blow—see a physician as soon as possible if the eye itself has been injured. A foreign body in the eye can usually be removed by touching it with the point of a clean, wet cloth; then wash with cold water.

Cuts and Abrasions should be cleansed with running cold water, then soap and water. Apply a sterile bandage, using hand pressure directly over the area if bleeding continues. For heavy bleeding, get medical attention immediately.

Heat Stress can produce cramps (which will usually respond to drinking diluted salt water), or more serious symptoms. It's important to remember that the body needs to be acclimated to heat, and that it may take a couple of months to be fully acclimated. Therefore, don't spend most of the summer in air-conditioned buildings and an air-conditioned car and then expect your body to react well to playing tennis in the heat. It won't. Also remember that the humidity is a large factor in heat stress, and that a temperature between 80 and 90 degrees with humidity more than 70 per cent is a very stressful situation for most people. You can easily collapse unless your heat-regulating mechanism has become accustomed to exercising in the heat.

As suggested earlier, salt tablets and lots of fluids (not a quart at a time!) will help prevent heat stress symptoms.

Heat Exhaustion if it occurs, requires prompt treatment. The player may feel confused and dizzy, and should be quickly removed from the court to a cool spot, as collapse may occur suddenly. Usually the face is pale and the skin cold and clammy. Give diluted salt water if the player is able to take it, and get medical attention.

Heat Stroke is a true medical emergency, failure of the heat-regulating mechanism. It may begin with weakness, headaches, and dizziness, or the player may suddenly begin vomiting with anxiety and muscular twitching. The face is flushed, the skin hot and dry, and the temperature elevated. The player must be cooled *immediately* and taken to a hospital for medical treatment.

In Your Tennis Bag you may want nothing more than a towel, a can of balls, and your racket if you are playing social tennis. But if you begin to play in tournaments, you'll gradually find yourself adding necessary items that you would have laughed at yourself for carrying at an earlier stage. For example, you can only play with one racket at a time, but if the strings break you're stuck. So an extra, of the same weight and grip size, is nice to have around. Add a couple of Band-Aids, an extra pair of shoelaces and socks, and a wrist band or two. Now put in a box of sugar cubes, a couple of small cans of juice or the equivalent, an anti-fogger for your glasses, and a packet of Kleenex. All set? One more thing—you almost forgot your hat and sunglasses.

SELECTED BIBLIOGRAPHY

Bowerman, William F., and Harris, W. E., M.D.: *Jogging*.
Grosset and Dunlap, N.Y., 1967.

Conroy, John J., and Kraft, Eve F.: *The Tennis Workbook—
Unit II*. Scholastic Coach Book Services, Inc., Englewood
Cliffs, N.J., 1969, p. 70.

Cooper, Kenneth H., M.D.: *Aerobics*. M. Evans and Co., Inc.,
N.Y., 1968.

Jones, C. M.: *Tennis: How to Become a Champion*. Faber and
Faber, London, 1968.

King, Billie Jean: *Tennis to Win*. Harper & Row, N.Y., 1970.

Kraft, Eve F.: *A Teacher's Guide to Group Tennis Instruction*.
Scholastic Coach Book Services, Inc., Englewood Cliffs,
N.J., 1969, pp. 43–46.

Lardner, Rex: *Beginner's Guide to Tennis*. Doubleday & Co.,
Garden City, N.Y., 1967.

Margaret Court Instructional Film Series. Scholastic Coach
Athletic Services, 50 W. 44th St., New York, N.Y. 10036.

Palfrey, Sarah: *Tennis for Anyone!* Simon and Schuster, N.Y.,
1972, pp. 106–17.

Physical Fitness Research Digest. President's Council on Physical Fitness and Sports, Washington, D.C., Series 3, No. 1, Jan. 1973.

The Prudent Diet. Department of Health, City of New York, March, 1965.

Royal Canadian Air Force Exercise Plans for Physical Fitness. Pocket Books, Inc., N.Y., 1962.

Ryan, Allan J., M.D.: *Heat Stress and the Vulnerable Athlete.* The Physician and Sportsmedicine, Vol. 1, No. 1, June 1973, pp. 47–53.

Steinhaus, Arthur H., Ph.D., M.P.E.: *How to Keep Fit and Like It.* The Dartnell Corporation, Chicago, Ill., 1963.

Swengros, Glenn and Monteleone, John J.: *Fitness with Glenn Swengros.* Hawthorne, N.Y., 1971.

Trengove, Alan: *How to Play Tennis the Professional Way.* Simon and Schuster, N.Y., 1964.

With the co-operation of the United States Lawn Tennis Association, Doubleday has published the following titles in this series:

Speed, Strength, and Stamina: Conditioning for Tennis, by Connie Haynes with Eve Kraft and John Conroy.
Detailed descriptions of exercises for tennis players, and suggestions for keeping in shape.

Tactics in Women's Singles, Doubles, and Mixed Doubles, by Rex Lardner.
A book for women tennis players, with specific suggestions for taking advantage of opponents' weaknesses.

Sinister tennis, by Peter Schwed.
How to play against left-handers and with left-handers as doubles partners.

The following titles are in preparation:
Finding and exploiting your opponent's weaknesses
Return of service
Covering the court
Ground strokes
Specialization in singles, doubles, and mixed doubles
The serve and the overhead
The half volley and the volley
Teaching tennis
Tennis as a therapy
Skills and drills

Each book in this series is illustrated with line drawings and is available in both hardcover and paperback editions.